# Restorative Justice:
# An Overview

by
Tony F. Marshall

A report by the Home Office
Research Development and Statistics Directorate

Restorative Justice: An Overview
by
Tony F. Marshall

Published by

Coventry Lord Mayor's Committee for Peace and Reconciliation
http://coventrycityofpeace.uk
https://twitter.com/CovCityOfPeace
https://www.facebook.com/coventrycityofpeace/
covlmpc@gmail.com
176 Greendale Road
Coventry CV5 8AY

on behalf of the Coventry Restorative Justice Forum
http://www.covrj.uk
https://twitter.com/CoventryJustice
https://www.facebook.com/covrj

**Publication History**
1999 published by the Home Office
2018 Published by Coventry Lord Mayor's Committee for Peace and Reconciliation

**ISBN**

| | |
|---|---|
| Paperback | 9781722256906 |
| eBook | 9781871281477 |

# CONTENTS

ACKNOWLEDGEMENTS ........................................................................................................ 4

RESTORATIVE JUSTICE: AN OVERVIEW ......................................................................... 5

    What is Restorative Justice?............................................................................................... 5

    What is Restorative Justice for?......................................................................................... 6

    Why is it called Restorative Justice?.................................................................................. 7

    How did the idea of Restorative Justice arise? ................................................................. 7

    Relationship of Restorative Justice to Legal Justice ......................................................... 8

    Limitations of Restorative Justice ..................................................................................... 8

    Organisations promoting Restorative Justice .................................................................... 9

    Examples of Restorative Justice practice ........................................................................ 11

    Research on Restorative Justice practice ......................................................................... 20

    Restorative Justice and crime policy............................................................................... 23

    Major issues in the development of Restorative Justice................................................... 26

    Theories related to Restorative Justice ............................................................................ 33

REFERENCES .................................................................................................................... 36

# ACKNOWLEDGEMENTS

I have received materials and information from a number of parties and am grateful for their generosity. They are too many to list here, but they, or their organisations, are mentioned in the text. I wish to record special thanks, however, to Annie Roberts for assiduously keeping me abreast of the American literature in particular, and for the general support and intellectual stimulation of Marian Liebmann and Martin Wright over many years.

Tony F Marshall

# RESTORATIVE JUSTICE: AN OVERVIEW

## What is Restorative Justice?

Restorative Justice is a problem-solving approach to crime which involves the parties themselves, and the community generally, in an active relationship with statutory agencies.

It is not any particular practice, but a set of principles which may orientate the general practice of any agency or group in relation to crime.

These principles are:

- making room for the personal involvement of those mainly concerned (particularly the offender and the victim, but also their families and communities)
- seeing crime problems in their social context
- a forward-looking (or preventative) problem-solving orientation
- flexibility of practice (creativity).

Restorative Justice may be seen as criminal justice embedded in its social context, with the stress on its relationship to the other components, rather than a closed system in isolation (see diagram below).

A commonly accepted definition used internationally is: Restorative Justice is a process whereby parties with a stake in a specific offence collectively resolve how to deal with the aftermath of the offence and its implications for the future.

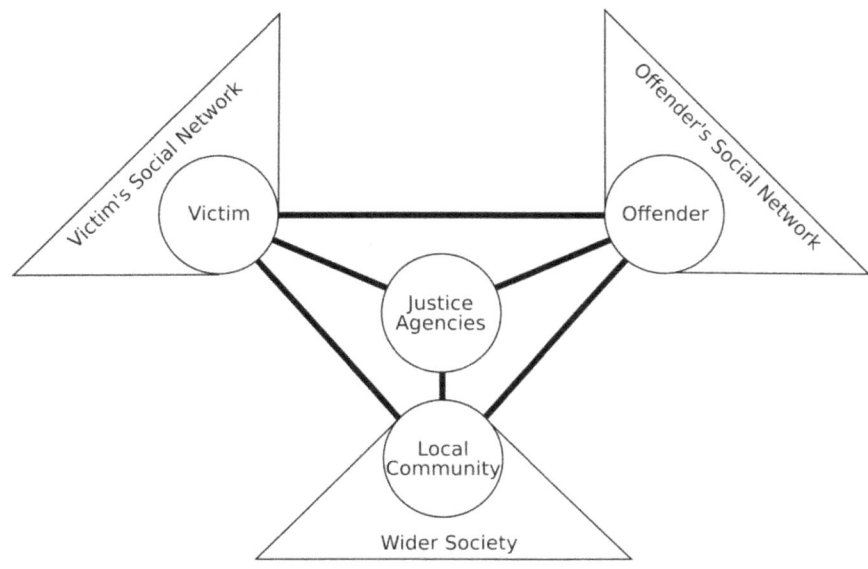

# What is Restorative Justice for?

The primary objectives of Restorative Justice are:

- to attend fully to victims' needs – material, financial, emotional and social (including those personally close to the victim who may be similarly affected)
- to prevent re–offending by reintegrating offenders into the community
- to enable offenders to assume active responsibility for their actions
- to recreate a working community that supports the rehabilitation of offenders and victims and is active in preventing crime
- to provide a means of avoiding escalation of legal justice and the associated costs and delays.

These might all be objectives of the current criminal justice system, and although primacy has been given in the new Crime and Disorder Act to the prevention of offending as the statutory aim of youth justice, the system only partially and haphazardly achieves this, or any other aim. It is not centrally concerned with victims and does not address most of their needs. Only limited action is taken to encourage the reintegration of offenders, and the evidence shows that this is largely unsuccessful. It requires only the passive acquiescence of offenders, who are not expected to take the initiative in making good what they have done but only to suffer their punishment. It is distant from the community and does little to encourage any role for it in the prevention of c rime. Despite various programmes intended to divert offences from the full process and reduce costs and delays, their use without parallel attention to victims' needs and future prevention has sometimes led to the criticism that much crime is not taken sufficiently seriously. (The new Crime and Disorder Act seeks to deal with this last point by eliminating the use of multiple cautions and instituting opportunities for victim consultation and preventive measures, an approach which is in accord with Restorative Justice.)

Restorative Justice is based on the following assumptions:

- that crime has its origins in social conditions and relationships in the community
- that crime-prevention is dependent on communities taking some responsibility (along with local and central governments' responsibility for general social policy) for remedying those conditions that cause crime
- that the aftermath of crime cannot be fully resolved for the parties themselves without facilitating their personal involvement
- that justice measures must be flexible enough to respond to the particular exigencies, personal needs and potential for action in each case
- that partnership and common objectives among justice agencies, and between them and the community, are essential to optimal effectiveness and efficiency
- that justice consists of a balanced approach in which a single objective is not allowed to dominate the others.

# Why is it called Restorative Justice?

Restorative Justice is centrally concerned with restoration: restoration of the victim, restoration of the offender to a law-abiding life, resto ration of the damage caused by crime to the community. Restoration is not solely backward-looking; it is equally, if not more, concerned with the construction of a better society in the present and the future.

Other terms have been used to refer to basically identical ideas (see Marshall, 1997 for a discussion of these). The Relationships Foundation (previously the Jubilee Policy Group) has used the term Relational Justice to emphasise the fact that this kind of justice is more concerned with the creation of positive relationships than traditional justice processes. Positive Justice was used by an eponymous group that advocated the same ideas as a means of moving away from the negative emphasis on punishment for its own sake to a more constructive approach to justice. Reintegrative Justice has also been used, both as a synonym for restorative and to refer more specifically to Braithwaite's (1989) theory of reintegrative shaming (see below, Theories of Restorative Justice).

The term Restorative Justice is not inherently better than any of the alternatives, but it has the longest history, is the internationally accepted term, and is the most commonly known in this country.

# How did the idea of Restorative Justice arise?

The first use of the term is generally ascribed to Barnett (1977) referring to certain principles arising out of early experiments in America using mediation between victims and offenders (see Wright, 1991, for more on the early history of the idea). These principles have been developed further over time, as commentators have thought them through and as other innovative practices have been taken into account, but their basic justification is still grounded in practical experience. Innovation in criminal justice has mainly been in response to frustrations that many practitioners have felt with the limitations, as they perceived them, of traditional approaches. In the course of their normal work these practitioners started to experiment with new ways of dealing with crime problems. Practice developed through experience of what worked in terms of impact on offenders, satisfaction of victims, and public acceptability. In particular, it was realised that the needs of victims, offenders and the community generally were not independent and that justice agencies had to engage actively with all three in order to make any impact. For instance, public demands for severe punishment, which those working to reform offenders found to be counter-productive, could only be relieved if attention was paid to victims' needs and healing the community, so that offender-rehabilitation could only occur in parallel with the satisfaction of other objectives. Similarly, the overloading of courts and other justice agencies was due to the increasing lack of capacity of local communities to manage their indigenous crime problems, so that escalating costs could only be prevented by agencies working in partnership with communities to reconstruct their resources for crime-prevention and social control.

Restorative Justice is not, therefore, a single academic theory of crime or justice, but represents, in a more or less eclectic way, the accretion of actual experience in working successfully with particular crime problems. Although contributing practice has been extremely varied (including victim-support, mediation, conferencing, problem-oriented policing and both community- and institution-based rehabilitation programmes), all these innovations were based on recognition of the need for engagement between two or more of the various parties represented in the diagram on page 5. Coming from very different directions, innovating practitioners found themselves homing in on the same underlying principles (personal participation, community involvement, problem-solving and flexibility). As practice is refined, so is the concept of Restorative Justice.

In the course of this development there has been much inspiration from examples of community justice still in use (or recently so) among other non-Western cultures, particularly the indigenous populations of such new world countries as North America (Native American sentencing circles) and New Zealand (Maori justice). These practices have particularly contributed to the development of family (or community) group conferencing (see below), and were effective in moving Restorative Justice ideas away from the relative individualism of victim / offender mediation practice, providing a new community- oriented focus. (A communitarian theme, however, was evident in the early development of mediation in the form of Victim Offender Reconciliation Projects, VORPs, which represented an attempt by close-knit religious communities in North America to decrease reliance on formal justice.)

## Relationship of Restorative Justice to Legal Justice

One of the prominent concerns both within and outside Restorative Justice has been the boundary between negotiatory practices and the workings of the criminal justice system. There are concerns that the due-process safeguards for rights, equality and proportionality could all be lost. There are also concerns that the power of judicial agencies might undermine and convert the aims of restorative practices (Messmer & Otto, 1992). Some have argued for completely separate and parallel systems, neither interfering with the other. Others have countered that this would not lead to Restorative Justice at all, because all it gained would be destroyed by the alienating and negative effects of Adversarial Justice.

It is, in fact, difficult to see how, in practice, two independent systems could co-exist. There is bound to be some influence each way, and therefore the problem cannot be avoided. Even though Restorative Justice involves a greater or lesser degree of devolution of control to individual citizens and communities, it is now generally accepted that Restorative Justice can and should be integrated as far as possible with Legal Justice as a complementary process that improves the quality, effectiveness and efficiency of justice as a whole. It is this concept of integrated or 'whole' justice (Marshall, 1997) which underlies the concept of Restorative Justice outlined on page 5. It is not just a matter of new and different practices, but of traditional practice too, informed by the same underlying principles. In this way the two processes reinforce one another to mutual benefit, and evolve towards a single system in which the community and formal agencies cooperate. It is in this context that issues of legality and control must be resolved (see below, Major Issues).

## Limitations of Restorative Justice

Restorative Justice practices rely in large part upon voluntary cooperation (but see the discussion on voluntariness below). If one party is not willing to participate, the range of options is reduced. If neither party is willing, there is no option but to let formal justice take its usual course. There is therefore no prospect of justice being wholly restorative and of formal justice being wholly replaced. Traditional justice forms will remain to deal with cases where Restorative Justice is inapplicable because of the circumstances, or fails through lack of cooperation or through failure to come to a mutually acceptable resolution.

This might seem a major drawback to Restorative Justice. Experience has indicated, however, that the majority of individuals offered a chance to participate would like to do so, and the rate of agreements is also high. Later failures to carry out agreements are, moreover, much lower than failures to pay fines or compensation ordered by the courts. Restorative practices are, by their nature, more accessible and attractive to individuals because they provide them with flexibility for manoeuvre and are more easily understood than legal procedures. They also offer benefits that the formal system offers less certainly or not at all.

Another limitation to any practice which attempts to involve communities is the available level of resources and skills. Communities are not as integrated as they once were. There is a greater emphasis on individual privacy and autonomy, and major social divides occur between cultures and age groups. Greater community involvement would inevitably mean increased education, training and practical resources, more in some areas than in others, (see Community under Major Issues, below.) A third, related, limitation for Restorative Justice is the existence of social injustice and inequality in and between communities. While problems such as these continue the degree to which communities can be supportive, caring and controlling is restricted. Social divisions also make voluntary participation less likely or less effective. If Restorative Justice involves the community as a major player, there needs to be a community. The degree to which effective communities exist depends largely on other social policies apart from criminal justice. There are implications for education, housing, community development, employment opportunities, welfare, health and environmental services.

The last two limitations are, of course, equally barriers to the success of crime-control by any system, retributive or restorative, and are therefore not reasons for not proceeding in a restorative direction, if this offers benefits in terms of victims' needs and the quality of justice.

Some people may conceive of Restorative Justice as applicable only to minor offences, which, if it were so, would be a major limitation. Again, practice has shown that there may be even more to gain by working in this way with serious crimes, especially in terms of victim benefits, but also in terms of prevention. Such practice would normally take place alongside criminal justice rather than as a replacement for it. Just as there are lower-order legal procedures for minor offences, so one may have to conceive of lower-order Restorative Justice practices for the same offences or for minor offenders in order to prioritise the cases where more effort may have a greater pay-off. This issue of parsimony and the danger of marginalising Restorative Justice practice is discussed further below (see Major Issues).

# Organisations promoting Restorative Justice

The Restorative Justice Consortium is a forum of national organisations concerned in some way with promoting restorative practices. They share a common interest in fostering a better policy environment for such practice and good standards of operation. The Consortium's aims are:

> "to influence policy-makers so that they take full account of the need for Restorative Justice;
>
> to disseminate information about Restorative Justice;
>
> to raise awareness of the benefits of Restorative Justice within the criminal justice system and among people at large;
>
> to recommend standards for Restorative Justice projects;
>
> to share information and experience between members of the Consortium."

Its work is mainly taken forward through separate subcommittees on publicity, training, research and standards. The standards group is known as SINRJ (Standards in Restorative Justice) and comprises many co-opted members representing the foremost thinkers on Restorative Justice in this country, together with an international advisory panel.

The lead agencies in the Consortium are Mediation UK and The National Council for Social Concern, who act as the central points of contact for the Consortium.

Mediation UK is the national voluntary umbrella body for mediation initiatives of all kinds and comprises practising mediators, mediation bodies and individuals or organisations with an interest in mediation. From its inception ten years ago as a formally constituted body (at that time called the Forum for Initiatives in Reparation and Mediation, or FIRM), it has played a major role in the development of victim-offender mediation in this country. For much of its history it was the only lay body promoting the idea of Restorative Justice. The only other groups active in this way ten years ago were religious foundations, notably the Society of Friends and the London Mennonite Centre, both instrumental in introducing ideas (and training) from the United States before the foundation of Mediation UK. Mediation UK does not advocate any one mode of operation, believing that variations in practice are necessary to adjust to local circumstances, but it promotes a single set of practice standards applicable to all kinds of mediation. Apart from information-sharing, Mediation UK provides training, accreditation, advice, coordination and a directory of mediation services (Mediation UK 1996). [Mediation UK, Alexander House, Telephone Avenue, Bristol BS1 4BS. 0117 904 6661.]

The National Council for Social Concern is a relative newcomer to Restorative Justice. It is an independent charitable foundation which has a base in, and strong links with, the Church of England. Its focus has always been on crime issues, particularly addictions to drink, drugs and gambling. It founded the Court Missionaries that were the forerunners of the present Probation Service. It recently decided to generalise its activity by making Restorative Justice its major strand for promoting criminal justice reform. Its work is both educational and facilitative (for instance it provides a venue for conferences and seminars, and is building a library of Restorative Justice literature). In day-to-day practice it maintains strong links with Mediation UK, and the two often act collaboratively. [National Council for Social Concern, Montague Chambers, Montague Close, London SE1 9DA. 0171 403 0977.]

Victim Support is not normally thought of as a Restorative Justice body, although it plainly is, given that it is concerned with the provision of community support for victims and promoting victims' interests in criminal policy. Unlike the two previous organisations, it does not represent Restorative Justice per se, or in its totality, as it is partisan on behalf of victims and its constitution prevents it taking a view on the treatment of offenders. Nevertheless, it exercises an observer role on the Consortium and is a key player in Restorative Justice thinking. Victim Support provided the facilities for the first informal meetings of the forum which eventually became Mediation UK, and the links between the two organisations have always been close. The Director of Victim Support, Helen Reeves OBE, was at one time a member of the Board of FIRM, and Martin Wright has been a prominent worker in both organisations. Many local Victim Support schemes have helped initiate mediation services in their areas, and they are represented on the steering groups for all victim-offender mediation services that are professionally constituted. [Victim Support, Cranmer House, 39 Brixton Road, London SW9 6DZ. 0171 735 9166.]

The National Association for the Care and Resettlement of Offenders (NACRO), like Victim Support does not define its activities solely in terms of Restorative Justice, and it is also partisan, its focal concerns being the welfare and rehabilitation of offenders and the welfare of their families. Nevertheless, it has been one of the main promoters of community-based support for the rehabilitation of offenders over many decades and a great innovator of progressive practice, themselves essential components of a Restorative Justice programme. In the last few years it has become actively engaged with community mediation and with family group conferencing (based primarily on the New Zealand model). In conjunction with the Family Rights Group it set up The National Steering Group on Family Group Conferences and Youth Justice. Its recent publication Three Rs ( NAC RO, 1997) advocated Restorative Justice. [NACRO, 169 Clapham Road, London SW9 0PU. 0171 582 6500.]

NACRO 's Scottish counterpart, The Scottish Association for the Care and Resettlement of Offenders (SAC R O ), set up the first victim-offender mediation programmes in Scotland (in Edinburgh and then in Glasgow) and still runs services in Aberdeen and Motherwell, along with community mediation projects in Edinburgh and Fife. [SACRO, 31 Palmerston Place, Edinburgh EH12 5AP. 0131 226 4222.]

The Jubilee Policy Group, a think-tank involved in 'Christian analysis of public policy', published Relational Justice in 1994. What was advocated was entirely consistent with Restorative Justice, although based on their own theory of the importance of relationships and the need to repair them (especially between victim and offender) in the aftermath of crime. The group has recently re-christened itself The Relationships Foundation. [The Relationships Foundation, Jubilee House, 3 Hooper Street, Cambridge CB1 2NZ. 01223 566333.]

The Howard League has been for a long time the main penal reform advocate in favour of more humanitarian policies, especially with respect to prisons. It is a member of the Restorative Justice Consortium, although it has not particularly presented itself as a Restorative Justice organisation. A recent annual conference 'Positive Justice', however, focused on Restorative Justice ideas, and its new endeavour in schools 'Citizenship and Crime Project' (see below) is clearly representative of the restorative approach.

Among statutory agencies, probation services and social services departments were long the main bodies practically involved with victim-offender mediation, sometimes with the active involvement of the police through multi-agency youth-justice panels. More recently, all three agencies have been instrumental in starting conferencing projects in different parts of the country. The involvement of these agencies was, until the new Crime and Disorder Act, on a local basis only. The Association of Chief Officers of Probation ( ACOP ) supported Restorative Justice practice in its document 'Probation Services and the Victims of Crime' (ACOP, 1996): "We encourage probation services to explore the potential for partnerships with other organisations, to develop mediation between victims and offenders, and reparation if practicable." They have issued a joint statement with Victim Support (1996) and have recently drafted a similar joint statement with Mediation UK. [ ACOP: Roger Ford, Lead Officer on Work with Victims, Shropshire Probation Service, Abbeydale House, 39 Abbey Foregate, Shrewsbury SY2 6BN. 01743 235013.]

Other organisations concerned with specific aspects of Restorative Justice are mentioned in the next section.

# Examples of Restorative Justice practice

It is convenient to discuss these in terms of the various relationships shown in the diagram on p.5.

## *Victim-offender*

Victim-offender meetings are organised to give offenders a chance to take active steps to make voluntary reparation to their victims. Such reparation extends much further than financial compensation. It includes an apology and an explanation of how the crime came about, and the offender has to listen to the victim's own story and respond to it. The exchange can be therapeutic for victims and usually has a visible impact upon the offenders, who have to face up to the reality of what they have done. Offenders can restore their own reputations, to some extent, through reparation, and can be better prepared for reintegration into mainstream society by having resolved their guilt in this way. Reparation may take the form of:

- financial payments
- work for the victim for a the victim
- work community cause selected by counselling course),
- specific undertakings (e.g. to attend a or
- a mixture of these.

The context of personal negotiation allows flexible adjustment of agreements to the parties' needs and capacities and a greater level of creativity than court processes. Some victims find it helpful to them to be able to offer forgiveness in return for the offender's atonement. Any unresolved difficulties between them can also be settled – e.g. how to behave should they meet one another in the street, any remaining bad feelings or fears, or continuing relationship problems (if, as often happens, they already knew each other). Such meetings deal with victims' emotional as much as material needs. After a successful meeting both parties can effectively draw a line under the experience. In many cases the victim also experiences satisfaction from influencing the offender away from crime – transforming a negative experience into something positive.

The social benefits of victim-offender mediation are:

- victims' needs are more comprehensively served, including the need to be consulted
- victim and offender are able to see each other as persons rather than stereotypes (a learning experience for both), and,
- offenders are more affected by the experience than by normal prosecution and punishment, while being given a positive motivation to reform and a feeling that society is ready to offer re-acceptance.

Such meetings have to be carefully facilitated by a skilled, specially trained mediator, whose prime tasks are to ensure a safe and comfortable environment and firm g round-rules for a fruitful exchange which is re-affirming and a positive learning experience for both parties. The mediator may be employed by the body offering the service, or may be a lay volunteer. Both staff and volunteers undertake the same training programme, which is specific to the task of mediation with victims and offenders. The skills required are not as for those of counselling, social work, legal negotiations, arbitration, or any other profession.

In this country, victim-offender mediation is usually offered by specially constituted programmes that are run semi-independently of criminal y justice agencies, although they are often managed by such agencies (probation or social-work services, police services, or inter-agency panels). Some programmes are community-based, and victim-offender mediation may be offered as a special service by community-mediation programmes whose other main caseload is comprised of neighbourhood disputes. Whatever the managing agency, there is usually a steering committee comprising representatives of community groups, Victim Support and criminal justice agencies. As mediators have to be respected and trusted by both victims and offenders it is crucial that their impartiality is protected.

Most victim-offender mediation services belong to Mediation UK and adhere to its practice guidelines and standards. This professional identity, shared with other types of mediation, is important for maintaining the impartiality and integrity of mediators.

As well as arranging direct meetings between victims and offenders, mediation services may negotiate between them if they do not want to meet or are unable to do so. This is usually described as indirect mediation. It enables flexible negotiation to suit both parties, but the agreement is usually limited to practical reparation and the transmission of an apology. Compared with a meeting, indirect mediation is less personal, does not allow victims' more emotional needs to be satisfied, is less effective in breaking down stereotypes and increasing understanding, and may be less influential in reforming offenders. On the other hand, for many victims not desiring a direct encounter it may be preferable to no involvement at all.

Victim-offender mediation may be offered in conjunction with a police warning or caution, with deferred prosecution, in parallel with prosecution (before court or between conviction and sentence), as part of a sentence, or after sentence. It is relevant to any offence however serious, as long as there is an identifiable victim (which may be a corporate body) and as long as the defendant admits causing the harm. Participation in mediation is always voluntary for both parties. Mediation may be initially suggested by an agency, the offender (or his/her legal representative), or the victim.

Apart from specific programmes, it sometimes happens that criminal justice officers have a chance to mediate between a victim and an offender in the normal course of their work. This may, for instance, be a police officer at a call-out to a domestic dispute, or a probation officer in the course of normal casework. While formally offered mediation services should be professionally organised and conducted by qualified staff or volunteers, such incidental or extempore mediation, still has its place as long as officers are aware of the limitations on what they can attempt with little time and experience, and from a position that may not be entirely impartial (or not perceived as such). An example of where this sometimes occurs and can be valuable is in social work with incest offenders, in which a meeting with the victim can help resolve remaining emotional problems when both parties have reached the necessary stage in therapy and emotional adjustment.

As well as negotiation between victims and their offenders, there have from time to time been programmes for groups of offenders who have committed similar offences to meet with groups of victims who have suffered the same type of crime. It is a way of being able to provide a service to victims whose own offenders are not caught or are unable to meet them. They get the same chance to express their feelings and to ask questions of the offenders. For offenders, it is also a chance to gain some insight into the personal effects of what they have done. Group meetings lack the immediacy and personal relevance of the one-to-one victim/offender meeting, but may still perform a useful communication function. Such programmes are usually carried out with groups of prison inmates or probationers. One is currently running in Long Lartin prison. The programmes have so far always been short-lived, partly because they appeal only to a small minority of victims.

## Victim-community

Community support for victims most often occurs through the victims' own personal acquaintances or relatives, and this is the most natural source of assistance and usually the most valued. Such assistance may, however, be less available to some individuals than others. The voluntary organisation Victim Support exists to fill this gap by offering practical help, support and consolation to victims on a local basis, using available trained lay volunteers to visit those who request it. By showing community concern, Victim Support helps to overcome the social distrust and sense of alienation that afflict many victims of crime. It helps resto re the victim materially, psychologically and socially. Moreover, volunteers' specialist knowledge of psychological reactions to crime may facilitate better support, in some cases, than from friends and relations who may fail to understand the victim's real needs (or have their own problems in coming to terms with what has happened).

Other community groups are also engaged in helping particular kinds of victim. These may, for instance, be women victims of domestic violence (e.g. Women's Aid), or children victims of abuse (Childline). There also exist self-help support groups for parents of murdered children, victims of drunk drivers, and so on. These voluntary organisations play a crucial part in resto ring victims and are an essential part of a functioning community.

Yet other groups may be concerned with helping to prevent victimisation, such as the Suzy Lamplugh Trust, which offers training in how to deal with violence and prevent its escalation.

## Offender-community

There is a multitude of projects in different communities, which attempt to help offenders of various kinds, whether in trying to find jobs, retraining, literacy education, relationships counselling, drug or alcohol counselling, mentoring, accommodation for the homeless, support for the isolated, or the provision of activities to release energies or encourage social integration. Other services support families to improve their parenting skills. Such provision is unsystematic and variable, but it is an expression of communities' feelings of responsibility for reincorporating their deviant members and supporting those that have been damaged by their experiences. Many organisations, such as youth clubs or adventure play grounds, perform a preventative function by their very existence. NACRO is a national organisation that provides many innovative projects in crime-prone neighbourhoods, and Community Service Volunteers [CSV, 237 Pentonville Road, London N1 9NJ 0171 278 6601], run mentoring schemes among many other programmes, but there are numerous other bodies engaged in rehabilitative or supportive work of this kind. It would be impossible to list them all, but The Society of Voluntary Associates (0171 793 0404) organises a great variety of volunteering opportunities for citizens who want to assist offenders, either in the community or in prisons. (See Utting, 1996 for examples in relation to young offenders. )

Rather than helping individuals or groups, a special group of programmes is concerned with helping communities as a whole become less crime-prone. NACRO's Safe Neighbourhoods work is an example attempting to improve the physical and social fabric of crime-prone neighbourhoods. They are special examples of economic and community development programmes generally which, by encouraging communal action and responsibility, and providing the resources for this (including the skills), enable communities to prevent and contain crime, as well as improving the quality of life generally.

Another group of programmes is engaged in schools. These are mainly concerned with incipient offending – programmes for bullying, truants, misbehaviour or school exclusions, for instance. They are often concerned with improving the capacities of schools to themselves deal with their internal problems – such as dispute- resolution training for pupils, which enables them to avoid trouble escalating from disputes, or even to provide their own mediation services for fellow pupils (Marshall, 1987). School-mediation programmes exist in a number of British schools and there are even more in the USA and other countries, such as Norway. Group meetings of family members, pupils, other parents, teachers and community members are being facilitated in some schools to develop programmes for supporting disruptive pupils who would otherwise have to be excluded. Other programmes are concerned with making children aware of their coming responsibilities as adults and citizens – parenthood training, drugs and sex education, and citizenship. An example of the latter, focused more specifically on crime, is the Howard League's Citizenship and Crime Project, in which conferences are held in secondary schools, led by volunteers from a variety of agencies to facilitate discussion among young people. School Outreach is a voluntary organisation training and placing counsellors in schools to improve pupil support and home school links.

Yet other programmes are concerned to help imprisoned offenders before they are released or on release, including work with prisoners' families, which may help to keep their social networks intact. Some programmes help violent offenders learn how to control their own violence and channel their aggression in a positive way (e.g. the Alternatives to Violence Project, AVP, which began in America and has been introduced into Britain). Some projects work specifically with wife-abusers. Other programmes help in a more general way to prepare for release in order to avoid the prisoner facing extreme social pressures of isolation and social rejection, or overwhelming feelings of inadequacy (e.g. Inside Out).

Similar programmes providing a wide range of interventions are operated in the community for persistent offenders in danger of being sent to prison, participation in which may be assigned as part of a community sentence by the court. There have been a large number of intermediate treatment programmes of this sort over the years, run by community organisations (such as Save the Children or Barnardos) or by multi-agency teams (e.g. the Kent Intensive Support and Supervision Programme, or Repeat Offender Project, which also offers community conferencing – see below).

The relationship does not have to be all one way. Offenders in some programmes carry out work for their own communities, which can help give the offenders a sense of social responsibility and an experience of social acceptance and recognition. Prisoners, for instance, may be allowed to carry out work on behalf of the community or make produce for sale in order to provide the pro fits to Victim Support (a kind of indirect reparation).

## *Victim, offender and community*

In traditional victim-offender mediation the community has a minimal role, except that the mediator may be a local community member. Occasionally victims choose to assume this kind of role during mediation, exploring with the offender how they might keep out of trouble in future or, on rare occasions, offering personal support. (In some cases the offender may be more obviously suffering than the victim.)

The community is given a more direct role in cases of group conferencing, which is essentially an extension of victim-offender mediation to include more parties – the offender's family, the victim's family or supporters (or several victims together), and community contacts of the offender who may be able to offer support or help (a teacher, employer, neighbour, youth-worker, church contact, etc). While the emphasis in victim-offender mediation is on the victim's suffering and how the offender may make reparation for this, the conference allows the offender's family (especially in the case of younger people) to share the blame and directly witness the harm caused, and, most importantly, allows an exploration not only of how the offender can atone, but also how to keep out of trouble in the future. It is equivalent to a case conference, where the offender's social network replaces the formal agencies and takes responsibility for exploring what has gone wrong, what steps the offender can take to reform, and how others can support him/her in doing this. As a force for social reintegration of offenders, conferencing is potentially a more powerful tool than one-to-one mediation, because it allows social resources to be brought to bear to ensure that the offender's change of heart is more likely to continue. While still addressing victims' needs, it also addresses those of the offender – and of society, that would benefit from his/her rehabilitation.

The first use of conferencing in New Zealand (Brown & McElrea, 1993; Hudson et al, 1996) demonstrated the possible problems – especially the difficulty of maintaining the focus on the victim when most of the participants were there because of their relationship to, and interest in, the offender (see Morris et al, 1993). Empowerment is also resisted by many families only too happy to leave responsibility for their wayward children to the system. Large groups of this kind also require even more skillful mediation than one-to-one encounters. While the mediator in the New Zealand system is a youth-justice work e r, and in the Australian version a police officer (a model emulated by Thames Valley Police in this country in their Restorative cautioning experiment – see Alder & Wundersitz, 1994), many argue that they should be neutral persons with specific professional qualifications for such a role. The skills required, in fact, are very similar to those required for other kinds of multi-party mediation utilised in this country and the USA for environmental, land-use and planning conflicts, and training is available in these skills. This would help avoid some of the procedural problems to which conferencing can give rise (as pointed out by Marshall, 1997b and Wright, 1997).

Like victim-offender mediation, conferencing can be used at different stages of the criminal justice process. In New Zealand it is used in conjunction with either a caution or a court appearance. In the latter, the offender and his/her family are charged with proposing a package of measures to compensate the victim and undertakings that will help prevent a repetition of the behaviour. If acceptable to the victim(s), this package is put before the court for ratification as a sentence. However, this involves the victim with a degree of responsibility for the sentence – which Victim Support in this country has considered an unfair burden.

Used in conjunction with a caution, the resulting agreement is not enforceable and more emphasis tends to be placed, as a result, on the process itself – especially (in the Australian version and in restorative cautioning) on the shaming of the offender. This process of shaming is based on the ideas of John Braithwaite (see below) and is meant to be reintegrative and not negative, but Braithwaite's theory held that shaming was only positive in its effects if it occurred within and by a community of people that the shamed person respected and was attached to. The artificial imposition of a shaming experience by agents of a statutory power does not seem to accord with that proposition, so it is doubtful whether such a process would be beneficial in its effects on future behaviour.

Given the greater resources needed to set up conferences, there may be arguments for prioritising them in terms of their likely usefulness (e.g. where there are indications of family dysfunction or of continued offending), and victims who are not related to the offender may prefer to take part in a simpler one-to-one meeting which focuses more clearly on their own needs, either instead of attending a conference (which could still proceed with the other members) or preceding it. (The new VOCS project in Inner London proposes to offer both services according to the circumstances of each case.) Conferencing is still a new technique in criminal justice and more experimentation is required. The inclusion of the victim in particular makes it very different from the kind of family conference with which social workers in this country are more familiar (especially for child protection issues; see, e.g. Lupton, 1998, who discusses family group conferences without once mentioning victims). In its combination of victim resto ration, offender reintegration, individual participation and community involvement, conferencing might be seen as a Restorative Justice process par excellence, but it is debateable whether it is either practical or desirable to meet all these ends at one time in the majority of cases.

Conferencing is in operation in this country in the Thames Valley and Humberside police areas (police-run, in conjunction with a caution along the Australian model), Hampshire and Kent (inter-agency initiatives, with youth-justice leadership, the latter using professional mediators from local community mediation services), Cheshire (a Barnardos initiative) and Inner London (an inter-agency initiative using lay volunteer mediators). While current conferencing projects are exclusively for juvenile offenders, there is no reason why the same principles cannot be applied to adults as well, as for victim-offender mediation (see Bowen, 1997, on experimental work with adults in New Zealand; see also McElrea, 1994).

In Canada, a model of conferencing has been developed explicitly modelled on native Canadian customs, which includes an even higher level of community involvement and control. This is known as circle sentencing and places the highest value on healing the community after crime (Assembly of Manitoba Chiefs, 1989). It is only likely to be relevant, however, to communities with a strong identity and a tradition of operating in this way. Similar practices occur as an alternative to legal procedure in many other countries that have indigenous populations with strong ancient traditions of managing their own concerns. One problem that these approaches encounter is the proclivity of many of their younger members to loosen their communal ties and become Westernised, so that the procedures have little power over them. This has happened with respect to traditional Maori clan-based practice in New Zealand.

Another strand of development has been Neighbourhood Justice Centres, which do not exist in this country, but are well established in North America, Australia and Norway (Municipal Mediation Boards). These receive referrals from the police, courts, etc., of cases involving disputes between parties. Mediation is carried out by trained independent mediators or a community panel. If successful, it allows for prosecution to be dropped. A good example is provided by the Community Justice Centres of New South Wales, which received over 5,500 referrals during 1996-97, of which 45 per cent resulted in direct mediation. Over 86 per cent of the latter ended in agreement. Referrals from courts were the most likely to be resolved (59% of all referrals). They have over 300 active mediators at any one time. (See Community Justice Centres, 1997.)

## *Justice agencies and victims*

The Victims Charter already embodies responsibilities on the part of all criminal justice agencies on behalf of victims, and represents a step towards the assumption of certain restorative ends. It is focused at present more on a voiding secondary victimisation (not making the victim feel even worse) than on providing positive help, although the latter is not entirely missing (e.g. providing information on victim-support services). A stumbling- block, at least in the context of prosecution, is that the victim has no standing as such, as against being a reporter or witness of a crime, until there is a conviction. Measures exist for awarding compensation, to be paid by convicted offenders on behalf of their victims, and these could be more widely used. The new reparation order has extended the capacity of courts to ensure that victims' needs are served in non-material ways as well.

Probation services have recently been charged with victim-enquiry work in the case of offenders serving longer prison sentences for personal crimes, helping them to avoid further trouble on release. In this context, some services with established mediation programmes have charged these units with victim-contact work so that they can offer mediation with the offender if relevant. This work extends the job of probation from its traditional offender-focus, to include more general responsibility for preventing trouble.

## *Justice agencies and offenders*

The main thrust of criminal justice has been to assign responsibility for criminal acts and allot proportionate punishments. It has not therefore been centrally concerned with reintegration of the offender. Attempts at reintegration are largely confined to the probation and social-work services. Their work is essentially restorative, effecting a link between offenders and the community through their work with families, help in gaining employment, referral to treatment facilities, encouraging community programmes for offenders, and so on. These important efforts, however, remain marginal to the main processes of justice, which may conflict with reintegration (for instance, incarceration, unless accompanied by a structured programme for release into the community).

Other agencies can, however, assist reintegration. Police in Thames Valley have attempted to introduce a more Restorative approach into their work with offenders who are not prosecuted through the use of restorative cautioning (based on conferencing practice). The Crime and Disorder Act incorporates similar features into the final warning system that replaces cautioning for young offenders. In Scotland there are mediation programmes accepting referrals from the Procurator Fiscal (the public prosecutor) of cases which, if satisfactorily settled between the parties, can be withdrawn from prosecution. Pre-sentence reports also help courts to assign appropriate sentences that might facilitate reform, although they often have limited options from which to choose. The greater use of community group conferencing could enable even more constructive packages of intervention to be incorporated into sentencing, including commitments to family, and community-support for the offender. The Scottish Children's Hearing Panels, moreover, provide a means of parental and community involvement at the court stage which could be employed towards more restorative ends. The government is in the process of introducing legislation to reform the youth court by introducing procedures inspired by Restorative Justice. This will be achieved by creating a new form of sentencing disposal for first-time offenders in youth courts who plead guilty. The disposal takes the form of a referral to a youth offender panel. The members of the panel will draw up a contract with the offender and his/her parents, aimed at tackling his/her offending behaviour and its causes. The panel provides a constructive forum in which to take account of the views of the victim, in a similar way to group conferences. Prisons, too, can be viewed punitively or restoratively. While most discourse on prisons has emphasised the deleterious effects of their regimes, it is possible to view them as positive assets to offenders, allowing them breathing space from involvement in those social relationships that reinforced offending, a chance to reconsider their behaviour, and opportunities to acquire the skills and knowledge for a new direction. (cf Bianchi, 1994; West, 1997)

Inter-agency partnerships can help iron out some of the clashes of aims that occur in the criminal justice system. A long-standing example is the Juvenile Justice Panel, that brings social work and probation knowledge to bear, along with justice considerations, in police decisions on prosecution. Probation work in prisons provides a further example.

The new Crime and Disorder Act will provide a changed context for this kind of work, with the emphasis it gives to the responsibility of the criminal justice system to be concerned with the prevention of offending.

## *Justice agencies and communities*

While criminal justice as a whole has been traditionally remote from the community, this has never wholly applied additionally to the police forces, which have always had a major peacekeeping and public-assistance role in support of the community. Public surveys have shown that this role is still highly valued. In the context of Restorative Justice, police community relations divisions would take on a more significant central role because active responsibility for developing good public relations would not rest with a small number of designated officers but would be part of the duties of every officer. (Marshall, 1992, collates a number of restorative initiatives from different countries.)

Probation services, too, have sometimes been seen as a link between criminal justice and the community, but the demands of casework have never allowed a major expansion of the probation community development role, which could be given higher priority within a restorative system. While police community work is more directly related to physical crime prevention, probation services could usefully encourage means for social crime-prevention.

Opportunities for volunteering in relation to criminal justice agencies provide another community link – lay visitors to police stations, boards of prison visitors, probation volunteers, special constables, prison-visiting, mediators for victim/offender programmes, etc.

Inter-agency partnerships can extend to collaboration between criminal justice agencies and community groups. This often happens now when agencies make use of community groups for rehabilitation programmes, or in problem-oriented policing. It occurs on a wider scale in Community Safety Partnerships, organised at local-authority level to bring together justice agencies, local authority departments and community groups in order to establish priorities that accord with local needs and to use a problem-solving approach to crime prevention. In this context there are possibilities for effective mediation between community groups (e.g. youth groups and householders). Such collaboration is similarly seen in the new Young Offender Teams. Probation services have often formed partnerships with community agencies to deliver reintegrative programmes for offenders (such as The Prince's Trust schemes to help offenders get work, learn skills or even start their own businesses). See Home Office, Sept.1997b, for examples of local authority partnership.

Community involvement has long been a feature of juvenile justice in Scotland, since the introduction of the Children's Hearings under the 1968 Social Work (Scotland) Act. Hearings are conducted before a lay tribunal of community representatives and include attendance by the offenders and their parents. Their remit is the best interests of the child rather than punishment (McAra & Young, 1997). There is, however, no role for victims in this system.

An innovative practice has been in operation in Vermont since 1995 – the reparative probation programme – where 'non-violent offenders are sentenced by the court to a hearing before a community reparative board (RB) composed of local citizens' (Bazemore & Griffiths, 1997). Victims, however, are rarely consulted at present, and the idea might be more applicable as a supplement to other practices (like victim-offender mediation) for victimless crimes.

Partnerships explicitly focused on Restorative Justice are increasingly under consideration, with examples in the USA (especially Minnesota and Maine, and, with respect to juveniles, Pennsylvania, Florida, New Mexico and Montana) and in this country (particularly the Milton Keynes Youth Crime Reduction Project, incorporating a number of interlocking initiatives).

# Research on Restorative Justice practice

## *Victim-offender mediation*

It is not possible to evaluate victim-offender mediation entirely in cost-effectiveness terms because it is primarily a matter of providing a fuller service to victims. There is inevitably a cost to enhanced service provision, but this is often justified in terms of its intrinsic worth – as in the case of Home Office funding of Victim Support. Does mediation offer a significantly better deal to victims to warrant the cost? National headquarters of Victim Support have recently taken an increased interest in mediation, although there is no firm policy line. Many local victims' services, on the other hand, have been instrumental in working in partnership with criminal justice agencies to set up mediation programmes, and are enthusiastic about what they can deliver to victims.

The earliest, and still the most comprehensive, evaluation of victim-offender mediation in this country was that carried out in the late 1980s by the Home Office in collaboration with a number of external research teams, published as 'Crime and Accountability' (Marshall & Merry, 1990; Marshall, 1991a). This showed that the majority of victims offered the chance of meeting their offender would like to do so. Moreover, having been given that opportunity the great majority (80%-100% in this and later studies) looked back on the experience as well worthwhile. There was some cause for concern, however, in a few programmes that tended to place pressure on victims to take part, or tried to rehearse their emotions to make a greater impression on the offender. Projects associated with divers ion from prosecution were the most prone to this problem. Documentation of this danger allowed development of better practice and the erection of safeguards against victims merely being used to make some impact on offenders. The national body Mediation UK has drawn up practice guidelines and has an accreditation scheme for mediation services. The inclusion of Victim Support on the management committees of such services is now standard practice.

## *Victim satisfaction*

Subsequent research, in this country and elsewhere, has confirmed the high levels of victim satisfaction with mediation (typically 75% or more), when this is carried out by services adhering to accepted standards (see e.g. Umbreit & Coates, 1992; Umbreit 1994; Umbreit et al, 1997). Satisfaction is often higher for those services that concentrate on direct victim-offender meetings, rather than those that carry out mostly indirect mediation (with the mediator meeting separately with the parties), but more information is needed on this issue (see Major Issues, below).

As a result of mediation, victims may feel less angry and fearful, feel personally vindicated, experience a degree of emotional healing, and be happy to witness that the offender has not been let off too lightly. In Umbreit (1994) and Umbreit and Roberts (1996) victims taking part in mediation were only half as likely to fear re-victimisation as those not doing so (although we cannot be sure there was no selection effect, whereby less fearful victims were more likely to participate in mediation). Many victims who take part may not have been deeply traumatised by the crime, but they still value the chance to be involved and to make some impression on the offender for the sake of potential future victims. This is the commonest reason for taking part in the case of corporate victims suffering recurrent crime. Some other victims are parents whose own children may have been in trouble and they appreciate that mediation would have been constructive for them.

## Completions

Completion rates for reparation agreements via mediation are very high (studies have shown figures ranging from 70 per cent to 100 per cent, compared with about 40 per cent to 60 per cent for reparation otherwise ordered). Thus compensation not only is more frequently obtained through mediation but also has a much greater chance of being paid than compensation ordered by a court.

While any victim may derive something of value from meeting the offender, those who have suffered deeply, especially from the more serious offences (e.g. violence, sexual assaults, household burglary or damage) have more to gain, so that mediation should be prioritised for such victims. Some victims may also be traumatised initially and not immediately capable of taking part in mediation, so that mediation should be offered on a flexible schedule, taking place when the victim is ready. This means that mediation should not be closely tied to criminal justice timetables. In many serious cases mediation may not happen until after sentence, for instance while the offender is in custody.

While mediation may primarily be a service for victims, it has been shown to have a considerable impact on offenders, and it is thought to have a preventative effect which potentially could make it cost-effective. There is currently no firm evidence that mediation is more or less successful for any specific type of offence or any age-group of offenders.

## Recidivism

The Home Office research, using matched samples of offenders, showed a small positive effect on recidivism. The effect held only for those having direct meetings with the victim. It is, of course, notorious that re-offending, especially over a short period, is a blunt tool for evaluation as there are many other factors that might affect continuation of crime. Observation of meetings, interviews with mediators and interviews with offenders showed that most offenders were considerably affected by the meetings at the time. They found facing the victim a difficult and emotional experience, and were particularly challenged by the fact that the typical excuses they might fall back on to explain away their behaviour could no longer be maintained in the face of the real suffering caused (see e.g. research by Messmer, 1992). Most offenders said that it was a harder experience than going to court, although they also felt more positive about themselves afterwards. Subsequent research has confirmed the power of mediation to influence offenders. The question remains, however, how long such an effect will last when offenders return to their usual haunts and associates.

Subsequent research in Britain has also shown small positive effects on recidivism (Dignan, 1992; Warner, 1993). The most recent results from a sample of 73 offenders during 1993-94, dealt with by the Leeds Victim- Offender Unit (all aged 17 or over), showed a reduction in the rate of reconvictions over two years of 14 per cent, from an expected rate of 54.2 per cent to 46.6 per cent. An experimental programme, for shoplifters only, in Milton Keynes (Retail Theft Initiative) was shown to have no effect on offenders who had a record ( McCulloch, 1997), although there was some evidence of more success with first-time offenders (always difficult to assess reliably because of the overall low expected reconviction rate) and the programme was popular with the shops. American research has shown positive effects in some cases and not in others, but the most recent study of four programmes (Umbreit, 1994) showed a 33 per cent reduction in re-offending over one year. It is not possible to know whether such differences are due to differences in the quality of different types of programme. Even if mediation is affecting chances of re-offending, however, there needs to be further support for its achievements to ensure they will be long-lasting.

## Costs

While mediation may in the long run be more effective in preventing crime than traditional criminal justice processes, there is not yet sufficient evidence of reductions in crime to see crime prevention as a major component of the cost equation. Costs per case for mediation vary with the type of organisation, seriousness level of cases, method of accounting, and whether or not volunteers are used as well as paid staff, but they generally range from £150 to just over £300. (Costs for the New South Wales Community Justice Centres are also within this range if one divides total expenditure by caseload; or about £500 per case resolved.) These figures compare with the average cost of a prosecution of about £2,500 per case (Audit Commission, 1996). Immediate savings in terms of other costs are therefore possible. The most thorough financial assessment of victim-offender mediation was carried out by Martin Knapp as part of the Scottish study by Warner (1993). This revealed that mediation was a cheaper option than the criminal process as long as caseloads reached a critical (but feasible) level. Dignan's (1992) research resulted in the same findings about cost-effectiveness for the Kettering Adult Reparation Bureau, although it was not as detailed an analysis as Knapp's.

These studies were of mediation in association with diversion, and there has been no equally thorough evaluation of the economics of those programmes that deal with cases that are still prosecuted. The Home Office research, however, included programmes dealing with prosecuted cases. This study showed that mediation had a considerable effect on sentencing patterns. Generally, there was a shift from fines to community sentences like probation or community service, as well as a large increase in ordering compensation. The drop in fines might have increased costs, although it may also have led to a decrease in fine- enforcement costs. There was also a small shift in sentencing away from custodial placements. This occurred to a sufficient extent to meet the total costs of the mediation programmes, because of the high costs associated with custody. While mediation parallel to prosecution, therefore, does not produce savings in criminal justice processing like the diversion schemes, it has the capacity to increase the likelihood of community rather than custodial sentences and therefore savings of another kind.

The most thorough financial assessment of mediation so far has unfortunately been restricted to neighbourhood mediation services. Dignan et al (1996) found that these services were cost-effective as an alternative to the time of local authority officers. The findings are very similar to the effects of mediation in criminal justice in association with diversion. What none of these economic assessments has been able to do so far, however, is to take into account the less material factors such as victim satisfaction, higher frequency of compensation paid to victims, public credibility, and effects on future crime rates.

## Family group conferencing

Conferencing is relatively new outside New Zealand and there is still no definitive evidence about victim satisfaction. An early New Zealand study (Morris et al, 1993) demonstrated a number of concerns in relation to victims – who were often side lined or not invited to meetings, or who may have felt overwhelmed by large conference s where everyone else was attending as relatives or contacts of the offender. This led to improvements in practice in New Zealand and the lessons have been applied in many of the new programmes being started in Britain and the USA (see e.g. Hudson et al, 1996; McCold & Stahr, 1996). The intentions of conferences, however, are more comprehensive than those of victim-offender mediation, and not solely focused on victims' needs, being more centrally concerned with addressing offending behaviour and its causes.

One of the shortcomings of victim-offender mediation is often that the offender's resulting commitment to reform is seriously attenuated by the lack of follow-up support. Such support, it is hoped, would come from conferencing, which is dedicated to working out a plan of rehabilitation for the offender and engaging the support of family and other acquaintances in helping the offender carry this out. It is too early, however, to have any evidence of the success of conferencing in this respect. Research is currently being carried out in New Zealand, Australia and North America, as well as in relation to several new conferencing programmes in this country (Thames Valley, Hampshire, Kent and Inner London). Early results from the Reintegrative Shaming Experiments in Canberra, Australia (Strang, 1997), indicate good rates of victim satisfaction, although lower than those for victim-offender mediation (72% were pleased that their case had been dealt with in this way, compared with 53% of those whose cases had gone to court). A study in New Zealand also found a marked difference in reconvictions between those who felt constructively involved in the family group conference and those who felt it had been a negative, shaming experience, the latter much more often going on to re-offend (Morris & Maxwell, 1998). This confirms the feeling of those involved in mediation and conferencing that the quality of the process is all-important.

## *Partnerships*

There is much research literature on the problems of partnership which indicates that the course of true love is never an easy one. Partnerships that are effective and enduring require skilled management, commitment and the investment of resources. The issue of agency leadership and consequent competitiveness is one of these issues, together with more general professional conflicts between agencies. Community groups also find it difficult to gain an equal voice with professional agencies and there is usually a problem finding realistic representatives (rather than token ones) and creating mechanisms for two-way communication between such representatives and their constituencies. These problems may best be resolved by investing management and facilitation support in partnerships, either through independent organisations with facilitation skills (the chair of meetings, for instance, might be independent, so that each party can concentrate on its own role and there is no obvious primus inter pares) or, as proposed in a Home Office paper (Sept. 1997a), through an inter-agency support group with full-time staff seconded for set periods from the main agencies. A failing partnership, or a superficial one, may do more damage to community confidence than no partnership at all.

# Restorative Justice and crime policy

Restorative Justice is not simply a matter of new self-contained programmes. It involves principles that can inform every aspect of the work of all criminal justice agencies. One can have restorative prisons, restorative policing, etc. Two key features are flexibility and creativity – having the freedom to respond in appropriate ways to specific cases and issues. Particular programmes tend to enlarge their scope and methods over time, so that differences between community mediation, victim-offender mediation and community conferencing can become totally obscured.

Research has shown that Restorative Justice programmes can be successful both in serving victims' needs and having a reformative impact on offenders. However, in the main current programmes are scattered and isolated from mainstream criminal justice work. Further integration with, and sharing of their objectives by, the police, courts, probation services etc would increase the likelihood that the gains achieved by mediation programmes can be sustained. At the moment, Restorative Justice programmes and mainstream criminal justice actions often pull in opposite directions. In some areas, such as Thames Valley and Kent, there have been attempts to align all criminal justice work with restorative principles, and such integration might be usefully encouraged more generally. This is consistent with the intentions of Youth Offender Teams and local crime prevention partnerships.

The principles of Restorative Justice are also compatible with general government social-policy objectives – namely, encouraging community involvement, personal responsibility, partnership and consultation. Restorative Justice practice has been developed at the grassroots by those working with offenders and/or victims and represents what has been found to work at that level. The principles have been derived from such experience rather than from any academic theory. The generation of Restorative Justice is therefore compatible with an emphasis on what works. While restorative approaches are sometimes seen as soft (because they encourage offender re-acceptance into the community), they have been demonstrated to be onerous in their demands on offenders to own up, apologise personally and take active responsibility for putting things rights – both in terms of helping their victims and reforming their own behaviour.

The assessment of Restorative Justice should not be carried out solely in terms of re-offending, however. The primary aim of many Restorative Justice initiatives is to provide a better service for victims (of which Victim Support is, of course, a prime example, involving expenditure which one would not attempt to justify in terms of its impact on crime), or heal and strengthen communities (with possible longer-term crime prevention effects). Some of the most effective initiatives are probably those in schools, which help to prevent exclusions and inculcate a sense of citizenship. These are again in line with government policies of early intervention and combating social exclusion, although they are not capable of short-term evaluation in terms of re-offending. Schools comprise the main community for children, and the major social influence apart from their families, and they do so, moreover, at the most formative stage in their personal and social development.

Restorative Justice programmes mobilise community resources (voluntary organisations, volunteer mediators), enhance community capacities for social control (conflict resolution, education, prejudice reduction, experience of collaborative problem-solving, etc) and directly create opportunities for offender support and reform (e.g. conferencing programmes). This approach has at least face validity as a way of tackling the root causes of crime, which are known to reside in the community and in early social experiences. Traditional approaches have removed crime control more and more from the community, and these have demonstrably failed to prevent a growth in incivility. Recent American research, part of the Project on Human Development in Chicago Neighborhoods, has shown that the main difference between low- and high -crime rate neighbourhoods was not poverty but what they termed 'collective efficacy', the degree to which there was mutual trust among residents and a willingness to intervene on behalf of the common good (Sampson et al, 1997). The rebuilding of community cannot be regarded as an easy task in modern society, with its emphasis on individual freedom and competition, but there is little disagreement with the proposition that crime will only be controlled ultimately by creating a greater sense of social responsibility and a caring society. While potentially cost-effective, such an approach is not cost-free; resources will be needed to bolster those neighbourhoods where sense of community is weak.

Insofar as new expenditure is involved, this will need to be justified in terms of benefits for:

- crime reduction
- individual victims and their families
- community strengthening.

While crime reduction may be a short- or medium-term achievement as a direct consequence, it may also benefit in the longer term from community strengthening. Greater satisfaction of victims' needs may also have longer-term benefits in terms of improving confidence in criminal justice, greater public acceptance of reformative crime strategies, and less demand for unconstructive punishments (which are themselves costly). Community strengthening, through its effects on fear of crime and increased feelings of being in control, should also contribute to confidence in the justice system.

There are inevitably initial costs to any programme of change, even one which is instituted in order to achieve economy. The extent to which these would involve 'new' money will depend on how far alternative sources can be exploited. As far as community-building programmes go, including those in schools, benefits for crime- reduction can potentially be achieved through non-criminal policies, depending on other government departments being persuaded to adopt programmes which are compatible with the needs of crime-prevention. Such programmes are not necessarily at odds with other social policy – community and citizenship programmes for schools might further education aims as well as crime-policy ones. Every pupil excluded from school costs local education authorities almost twice as much as one attending school, so that prevention of exclusion s makes sense, both economically and in crime-prevention terms. It seems sensible that school-based initiatives (to carry on with that example) should be integral to a coherent educational policy, rather than tacked on to organisations as part of a criminal policy initiative. The treatment of crime as if it were something existing completely separate from the rest of social life is one of the reasons for the ineffectiveness of current crime control. Community mediation (which has crime prevention pay-offs) is largely funded by local authorities to save costs to housing and environmental health departments, and similar arguments apply in other policy areas.

With respect to the expansion of Restorative Justice programmes within criminal justice, there will be developmental, training, and accreditation start-up costs and continuing staff and administration costs. Research on programmes associated with diversion has shown that those with caseloads that optimise the use of resources (about 200 or more per annum) will pay for themselves in reduced process costs to criminal justice agencies. Those programmes that do not involve diversion may also have direct savings if they facilitate the use of community sentences rather than custodial ones. Some of this funding may be capable of diversion from current criminal justice expenditure, but this will depend on a shift of overall practice in a restorative direction, allowing expenditure priorities to be shifted accordingly. Initially at least, the total cost of Restorative Justice programmes is not likely to be bearable from current agency budgets alone. In the longer term it should be possible to afford ongoing costs from consequential savings. It also has to be borne in mind that funding of such programmes is an investment that brings in the uncosted resources of voluntary organisations, partnerships and volunteer practitioners. These resources represent major added value. The Crime and Disorder Act implies the development of some services to underpin measures like the reparation order.

The adoption of restorative aims as part of the basic mission of all criminal justice agencies, and the creation of appropriate work practices in accordance with these, is a matter of assigning priorities and should not in itself be a major cost, apart from initial needs for reorganisation, planning, and retraining. Although some local services are already moving in this direction, a comprehensive change will demand significant impetus and guidance from central government.

Inter-agency partnerships, and community participation in them, are already being developed. As an addition to current workloads, they also involve extra expenditure or opportunity costs. Such collaboration is not achieved without some effort and time; there are always obstacles to overcome as much research has shown. The costs of facilitation and training for partnership need to be considered. Insofar as these measures are already going ahead, however, the adoption of Restorative Justice practice does not involve any additional financial demands.

All these developments would need support of various kinds, other than direct funding. Facilities will need to be provided for: training)

- development of mediation and conferencing programmes (advice, consultancy,
- training of personnel to work in such programmes
- accreditation of mediation and conferencing programmes
- training of criminal justice personnel in the use of such programmes Justice aims
- advice and consultancy to justice agencies on the adoption of Restorative
- training of agency personnel to incorporate restorative principles into their own work

- facilitation of community partnerships and consultation, including confidence-building and conflict resolution where necessary
- training of justice personnel in partnership working
- research monitoring of new developments to inform their gradual improvement
- some means of judicial oversight of informal settlements
- complaints mechanisms for individual participants
- public education to ensure understanding of the reforms and their rationale.

Given the radical nature of such a programme, there would have to be a phased programme of development. While agencies could be expected to adopt a restorative approach quite quickly, this will take time to percolate through their entire practice, especially as spending budgets are set one year or more in advance. Different services will move at a different pace. Restorative Justice programmes, in those areas which do not have them at present, would also take time to set up and bring into operation. Community involvement in particular will be a matter of gradual development. While specific pilot areas might be identified, and provided with research resources to e valuate their success, other services (and local authorities) will also be minded to develop similar programmes themselves (as several are already planning). Such a phase of disparate development has advantages for monitoring and assessment, enables the growth of standards and experience, and prevents precipitate commitment to ways of working that ultimately prove less viable. There would be no advantage to the imposition of a single centralised model from the outset, and the pace of development should be sensitive to the need for gradual readjustment in agencies' and public attitudes.

# Major issues in the development of Restorative Justice

Much of what can be included under the general principles of Restorative Justice throws up no special concerns, but the core of restorative practice, and what is most innovative about it, is concerned with the breakdown of the barriers between legal processes (the 'criminal justice system') and community action, including the introduction of personal involvement in what are generally impersonal, highly regularised, often bureaucratic, procedures. It is this aspect of Restorative Justice which raises a considerable number of fears and concerns a round justice, ethics, good practice and fairness. There are fears on the part of criminal justice agencies that the safeguards and protections of the law may be eroded. There are equally fears on the part of the promoters of restorative practice that it may be misapplied and abused by other practitioners (cf. Messmer & Otto, 1992). There are fears within the 'victims' lobby' that victim involvement will be encouraged for the sake of benefits to offenders (e.g. see Davis et al, 1988), while others fear that making victims' concerns and community views more central will increase the punitiveness of criminal processes. A Council of Europe committee is currently drawing up a set of recommendations and guidelines on these issues (Committee of Experts on Mediation in Penal Matters, PC-MP, reporting to the European Committee on Crime Problems, CDPC, Strasbourg; contact the British representative Tony Marshall for more details). See also Van Ness (1997) for a good discussion of legal issues from an American perspective. The Restorative Justice Consortium in Britain has adopted the statement of principles developed by SINRJ (see above), 'Standards for Restorative Justice', and this paper is available from the RJC (c/o Mark Thrush, Social Concern, Montague Chambers, Montague Close, London SE1 9D A ).

## *Defendants' rights*

Legal processes provide a great many protections to defendants, both against wrongful conviction and disproportionate punishment. If these are re m oved, for instance by diversion from prosecution to a family group conference (even when this is dependent on the defendant's voluntary agreement), there is the possibility that innocent defendants may plead guilty to avoid a prosecution and that any accused person may be led to accept an excessive burden of punishment. The probability of either of these occurring in practice is low, but the possibility that they might do so in particular circumstances demands certain safeguards. The latter may lie in good practice guidelines (internal regulation) or in legal advice and judicial oversight (external regulation). An example of internal regulation would be the provision that mediators or facilitators should be neutral as regards the case in hand, that they should be properly accredited, and that they should be concerned with protecting against the dominance of any one party in negotiation. More is said on good practice below. No matter how well established such practice may be, however, there is still a need to ensure that it is always observed and to demonstrate that it is being observed. Provision of opportunity for taking legal advice may help defendants take sensible decisions on participation and on the final outcome, but they cannot ensure that they do. Ultimately there is no alternative to some form of judicial oversight, although this would be excessively costly in every case. Processes of appeal or complaint should therefore be established for any party who feels they have been unfairly treated. Moreover, agreements for all cases above a certain level of offence–seriousness should be automatically reviewed by a court. Community-based processes should never have access to the use of force or extreme sanctions – such as incarceration or physical punishment.

## *Victims' rights*

Victims have a right to justice, and a right not to be further damaged (secondary victimisation) by the processes of dealing with the offence. Their right to justice includes the expectation that offenders will be appropriately dealt with and the wrongness of their actions condemned. Participation in mediation may help victims to achieve this even more surely than if the case is left to normal justice processes, and it may also serve their other interests, of which a court takes no cognisance. Nevertheless, there is also the possibility of this not happening, and they may feel aggrieved at the outcome. The relevant safeguards are the same as those above with regard to defendants' rights – good practice, complaints procedures, and judicial oversight of the more serious cases. With regard to secondary victimisation, participation by the victim in any process (other than when required as a court witness) should always be voluntary; ie victims should themselves be allowed to determine whether or not the potential benefits of any course of action outweigh the likely costs. To do so they need to be provided with full, unbiased information on the possible benefits and disadvantages, a chance to ask questions, and time to decide. These, again, amount to good practice among mediation services. Victims should also be provided with options for action that allows them scope to adjust their degree of involvement to the possible benefits to themselves – e.g. indirect mediation (without meeting the offender), a meeting with the offender, or participation in a group conference with members of the offender's family. Victims should not be faced with unfair choices such as 'a conference or nothing'. Equally, the timing of mediation should be appropriate to the victim's progress in emotional readjustment, not determined by the convenience of justice agencies or offenders' interests.

## *Voluntariness*

The principle of voluntariness has already been seen to be important with regard to parties' rights, but it has a deeper importance to Restorative Justice. If processes are to be restorative for either party, any direct participation must be willing and free, with respect accorded to each, so that they feel committed to an outcome that they feel they have had a full part in determining, and so that they feel the process has been fair and considerate. Research on parties' attitudes after mediation (e.g. Umbreit, 1994) reveals that victims more often perceive mediation as fair than they do the court process. This is almost certainly because they have been given a chance to have their say and to have their personal needs taken into account. If victims are to feel that the process is fair, voluntary participation is essential.

Offenders, too, must participate willingly if they are to be positively influenced by the process, although there remains the question how voluntary their voluntary participation needs to be. Given that a personal encounter with the victim is something few miscreants will be positively enthused about, some persuasion to take that route is not unreasonable, nor harmful, as long as involvement is ultimately willing and active. The offender, because of his/her actions, has an obligation towards the victim, and it is reasonable to expect some attempt to take responsibility and offer reparation. For the sake of the victim, persistently antagonistic offenders should not take part in direct mediation; it would in any case achieve more harm than good for both parties.

## The balance between victim and offender

The last paragraph has indicated that the parties in victim-offender mediation (unlike most other forms of mediation) are not to be considered balanced or equal. With admission of an offence, the offender has assumed the obligation to make good. This even applies where the offence has arisen out of a dispute with the victim, in which the victim may have been equally to blame or even more at fault. Any underlying dispute can only be dealt with when the current offence has been atoned for, when the bargaining table is once again level.

The balance between the parties is also important with respect to the selection of cases for mediation. Most Restorative Justice programmes have been instituted by criminal justice agencies. Their main concern in doing so is usually to have a greater impact on offenders, to justify dive r ting the offender (either away from prosecution or to a community sentence rather than imprisonment), or to decrease the cost of dealing with the offence. While these agencies also perceive it as an advantage that they may thereby be able to provide greater satisfaction to victims, this is not usually their dominant motivation. Cases are therefore normally selected according to the characteristics of the offence, the offender, or the stage in the process that the case has reached. Although many programmes also admit referrals from the victim, the opportunity for doing this is small, because the victim will usually not know when an offender has been caught. Research (e.g. Marshall & Merry, 1990) has confirmed that practice tends to be biased towards the interests of agencies or of offenders, rather than victims, even when it is conducted extremely fairly, purely because of a bias in selection. Any consideration of a nationwide adoption of mediation in criminal justice will therefore have to take into account that the primary concern of such services should be to serve the interests of the victim – otherwise there is no reason why victims should agree to participate in them. And if this is so, then all victims should be able to a vail themselves of such an opportunity if they wish, not only those whose offenders happen to be of the right age, type, or stage. This would mean that all offenders should be offered the chance to make reparation and all victims offered the chance of participating, whatever legal course is to be taken with respect to the offence. This leads to a further problem of prioritisation.

## Prioritisation

In the early days of the development of Restorative Justice programmes, before caseloads built up to current levels, there was little need to prioritise. It is now evident, however, that it would not be possible to offer full mediation services to all those who might opt for it (60% of victims would choose to meet their offender on the basis of current experience, and this ratio could rise if services became more prevalent and accepted). The problem of how to prioritise is one that is not currently resolved, but it will have to be confronted more and more as services expand. (One of the most recently established projects, the VOCS programme in Inner London, has explicitly set down selection criteria at the outset in order to economise resources and ensure they go where most needed – and the Leeds Victim-Offender Unit also has a written policy.) As stated above, it is difficult to justify presenting some victims with the opportunity and others not merely on the basis of the characteristics of their offenders. While great consideration will yet need to be given to this problem, it may be that a great deal of informal victim consultation and negotiation work will need to be carried out by main grade officers of the various agencies, leaving referral of those cases which demand more time, effort or skill than can be provided in that way, to more formal, professionally–run services. It is already true, for example, that police officers spend some time mediating in disputes and probation officers are able to arrange reparation informally for some of their charges. This effort does, however, need to be backed up by appropriate training for the various professional groups, both as a grounding in simple negotiation techniques, including issues sur rounding contact with victims, and an understanding of when more substantial intervention needs to be offered. Practices should become visible and recognised, so that good operating standards can be applied and approved by appropriate bodies (such as Victim Support). Eventually, national standards will need to be developed to guide referral decisions to ensure both economy and optimal effectiveness. Mediation services, too, may have to adopt fast-track and intensive programmes to react to lower and higher priorities. One of the major factors in determining whether a victim-offender meeting should take place may need to be the degree of importance this has for the victim. In order not to discriminate against offenders, they could all be given a chance to offer reparation (to the victim or to the community), and, if their circumstances warranted it, they could be offered a family group conference (which need not include the presence of the victim).

## Applicability

The issue of prioritisation raises the further issue of those cases where restorative approaches are most suitable. There has been a tendency for people to see them as less appropriate for serious offences, those committed by older people or by offenders with a record of crime. There is little basis for these views, however. Mediation services, for instance, have been as successful with adults as with juveniles, and generally with recidivists as with first-time offenders. There is usually more at stake, and therefore more to gain, in relation to serious crimes, and victim referrals usually involve more serious offences. Mediation is just as likely to prove successful in serious cases as in minor ones (although a higher proportion of victims may be unable or unwilling to take part). As stated above, any limitation according to the type of offence or offender could be against the interests of victims. Limitation to minor crimes also reduces the cost-effectiveness of restorative measures. New services may sensibly concentrate at first on less serious cases as they acquire experience, but there are strong reasons for removing restrictions as skills and resources permit. The success of restorative measures is dependent on more personal considerations, such as parties' attitudes, feelings, motivations and social situations, than on formal characteristics like age or legal offence.

## Stage of application

There has been no noticeable difference in the relevance of mediation at the various stages of the criminal justice process. A strong reason, moreover, for not limiting the applicability of such services to any one stage is to enable them to be provided at the time that is most suitable for the victim, when emotions are not too uncontrolled but still relevant – this may be quite early after the offence for many crimes, but several years later for the more traumatic, like rape. Timing depends very much on the personal characteristics of the victim and how quickly they are able to adjust to what has happened to them. In order that reparative measures do not arrive too late for many victims, consideration of the need for them would ideally be given at the earliest possible time after admission of the offence, with the timing of any action thereafter dependent on the views of the victim(s).

## Delays

One anxiety about restorative measures is that they might delay the normal legal process, about which there is already concern. Delays due to administrative procedures and workloads, however, should be differentiated from delays occasioned by productive work, which may serve victims and reduce the likelihood of further crime. While some services at the moment are geared to particular stages of the process (e.g. between conviction and sentence), there would be two benefits from relieving them of such time-constraints. One would be that criminal justice processes could continue at their normal pace (with or without feedback from restorative programmes); the other would be that timing could respond more flexibly to victims' needs and to the circumstances of the cases (some of which would benefit from more extended intervention). The main disadvantage would be that criminal justice decisions might have to be made without information from progress on private negotiation; although that would be no worse than the current situation. There could even be advantages in removing the direct link between decisions in the two processes. Where it was felt to be important to take mediation into account, deferments could be used in the public interest.

## Punishment

There has been an impression in some quarters that restorative measures are soft. This may be associated with their being more concerned with personal issues than with social judgements, allowing offenders more of a voice, and being orientated more towards prevention than sanctions in their own right. Some programmes have also been associated with diversion from prosecution or incarceration, and this may also have given the process as a whole a flavour of leniency. If, however, 'soft' is defined as ineffective, it can be more viably argued that current measures are soft, even when they involve draconian punishments. Restorative measures are tougher in several senses: they expect active responsibility on the part of the offender, including facing up to their victims and making reparation; they pay more attention to victims' needs; they pay more attention to what needs to be done to prevent re-offending (tough on crime). Excessive punitiveness does not equate with being tough on crime. Punishment works most effectively when carefully measured and accepted by all parties (offender, victim and community) as appropriate. Restorative programmes allow for a more flexible approach to sanctions in order to maximise their relevance for all concerned. Their more prevalent adoption may reduce overall punitiveness in favour of more effective reduction in the harm done and re-offending. Severe punishments may also involve high costs (e.g. incarceration, close supervision) that may not be warranted by their achievements, except when public protection is at issue, or as part of a deliberate plan for rehabilitation.

## Mediation and reparation

There is a strong relationship between victim-offender mediation and reparation, but they are different entities. Mediation is a process that enables various ends to be fulfilled, according to the needs of the parties involved (including the community generally). While material reparation to the victim would norm ally be one of the outcomes of this process, there are some victims who wish to forgo this, happy with an apology and explanation, and perhaps agreements for the offender to carry out some community service or address the causes of their behaviour. Such outcomes are still reparative for those victims, and the mediation process itself may also be directly reparative by allowing the victim to achieve emotional and psychological satisfaction. On the other hand, there is no need for material reparation to wait on mediation. An offer may be made and negotiation carried out without a meeting between the victim and the offender, and this may even provide conditions of trust that make a meeting more acceptable and more productive. Sometimes meetings are arranged for compensation to be handed over. There is no need to stick rigidly to the model that direct mediation should always precede material reparation, although the quality of the experience for the victim and the offender is generally better if they are able to meet earlier in the process. It needs to be borne in mind, moreover, that material reparation may not be the most important benefit for the victim, and its negotiation is not necessarily the final outcome.

## Justice and fairness

Another major concern about restorative measures is that they remove some decisions to the realm of private negotiation and may therefore prevent equal treatment of all offenders, or justice in the legal sense. On the other hand, the general public often sees apologies and reparation as an essential element of complete justice, and mediation programmes are more often seen as fair by victims taking part than is the court process. Strict legal justice, re m oved from public participation, may be seen as partial and insufficient, leading to demands for greater severity as the only way in which victims and the general public are currently able to have a voice. Victims may not feel any sense of justice when their needs have not been met (except, vicariously, a desire for revenge). The public may not feel any sense of justice when most offenders continue their criminal careers despite prosecution. There are, of course, issues about offenders' and victims' rights, but these have been dealt with above. With appropriate judicial oversight, restorative measures may provide a fuller sense of Justice.

## *Organisational location*

Many different agencies have initiated restorative programmes. There is often a strong sense of ownership, which may inhibit more extensive partnership and reinforce the maintenance of control against the interests of neutrality essential to, for instance, mediation. While any agency may properly take the lead in promoting restorative practice, services themselves, particularly where victims are to be involved, should be independent and overseen by an inter-agency committee which includes community representation. All agencies should be encouraged to make use of the provision. Although mediators should be employed specifically to carry out that job, and not have other criminal justice responsibilities, this does not preclude some of them having backgrounds in criminal justice work of any kind, as long as they are specifically trained. There would be great advantage in staff secondments to mediation programmes (for periods of, say, two years) in order to increase understanding of such programmes in all the agencies concerned. Returning staff would be particularly useful in leading agency practice generally in a restorative direction.

## *Good practice*

Mediation between people who have been divided by crime is one of the most skilled and sensitive tasks to which anyone could be assigned. This is even more so when that mediation involves further parties, as it does in the case of conferencing. Training is essential in the relevant skills (which are distinct from, but overlap with, counselling and social-work skills) and in the philosophical orientation necessary for a role as a neutral party. Not only is intensive training necessary, but mediators must also be selected for their ability not to take sides, their empathy for different kinds of people, patience, ability to control the essential conditions while empowering the parties to take control of the content, ability to remain calm and uninvolved when emotions are on display, and mental agility. Such skills have been found to be widely spread across the population and are by no means related to educational level. Skills are developed, after training, through practice and professional discussion in a continuous process of self-improvement. With confidentiality, physical safety and legal issues at stake, programmes require good supervisory, management and record-keeping structures. Mediation UK has developed codes of good practice over many years which are as good as those in any other country. They also offer accreditation for mediation programmes. A comprehensive handbook for developing good practice is provided by Quill & Wynne (1993).

## *Direct and indirect mediation*

Mediation is usually presented in terms of direct meetings between victims and offenders. This is meant to be empowering for the parties, in that they can keep control of their own dialogue, which cannot happen through a go-between. It also allows the parties to have direct experience of each other, to make their own judgements, to express themselves directly and to have a more meaningful and emotive experience. This ideology contrasts to a reality where most mediation in this country is conducted without a face-to-face meeting. (This is not so in other countries, where direct mediation is the preferred mode of operation; Community Justice Centres in New South Wales, for instance, have an 85 per cent rate of direct mediation.) The reasons for the high rate of indirect mediation in Britain may be:

- reluctance among most victims to meet their offenders directly (although it is difficult to see why there should be such a vast difference between British victims and those elsewhere, and it does not accord with public surveys where the majority of victims would opt to meet their offender; moreover, some British programmes have achieved high rates of direct mediation);
- mediators being excessively concerned not to be seen to be putting any pressure on victims to take part, or being over-cautious;
- mediators subconsciously preferring indirect mediation because it leaves them in control, and is quicker and simpler to carry out.

Insofar as victims are sure they do not want to meet their offenders, then indirect mediation is obviously the only option, but the low rate of direct mediation in many British programmes may mean that many victims who would have gained more advantage from a direct meeting are being denied the possibility. It has to be remembered that many victims may be dubious about the idea at first but in retrospect are usually pleased to have taken part. Victim satisfaction rates are higher in relation to American victim-offender programmes than British, and this may be connected with their higher rate of direct mediation (Umbreit & Roberts, 1996). It is also to be expected that direct mediation would have more effect than indirect on the offender. (The Home Office research reported in Marshall & Merry, 1990, found that only direct mediation generally reduced recidivism. Research by Wynne & Brown, 1998, in relation to the Leeds Victim-Offender Unit, which purports to demonstrate the opposite, is based on too small a sample and inadequate controls.)

A further consideration, however, is that of economy. It may be sensible to limit the rate of direct mediation in order to prioritise those cases where a meeting will be particularly beneficial. This issue requires further investigation through independent research, but in the interim the basic principles guiding practice might be:

(1) any victim who is likely to derive more benefit from meeting the offender, and who is prepared to do so, should be enabled to do so, subject to the offender's agreement and the mediator's judgement that such a meeting would be manageable and safe;

(2) victims should be given full information about the possible advantages and disadvantages of a meeting in order to make up their own minds.

## *Confidentiality*

What passes during mediation sessions is normally completely confidential, unless the parties agree otherwise. This limits the information that can be passed to justice agencies to the fact that mediation has (or has not) taken place, and the outcome (a copy of the agreement). The exception to this would be information about the possibility of a future serious crime. Agencies (e.g. courts) might prefer to have fuller information than this – for instance the offender's attitude and willingness during the process – but such information might be subjective and unreliable, and the condition of confidentiality is essential for the free sharing of views required for effective mediation. While the mediator is under strict limitations with regard to confidentiality, there can, however, be no guarantee that one or other of the parties will not reveal such information. (Or that they might not use information gained during the mediation for their own ends.) This danger should be spelt out clearly to parties before entering the process, as it may affect their participation or the conditions of participation (e.g. a victim may not want to meet the offender at the former's home, in case the offender should choose to victimise them again). Mediation services also need to be alert to this danger and avoid direct mediation where it might lead to problems. There is a further issue with regard to conferencing, when representatives of criminal justice agencies may well be present and thus privy to the information that is shared. Again, it is important that parties are aware of the possible implications of this before agreeing to go ahead. Parties may therefore be more reticent in a conference than they would be in a private victim-offender meeting.

## *'Community'*

As with any initiative that invokes 'community' it is necessary to think about what this may actually involve. Neighbourhoods differ in their capacities to support potential offenders in their midst. Programmes that seek to tap into community support may therefore be tapping into something that hardly exists. In the more broken communities, resources and education may need to be committed for Restorative Justice programmes to work. Otherwise there is the danger that such programmes will increase the burden of expectation and involvement of local people and groups to a level they cannot sustain. Initiatives like conferencing, therefore, may need to be introduced gradually and in parallel with the development of other community programmes. Similarly, work in schools may be hampered if the schools have few spare resources, particularly of uncommitted time. (cf. Crawford, 1997.) At the same time, 'community' does not have to correspond to any particular physical or geographical entity. For the purposes of conferencing and so on, the circle of relatives, supporters and significant others that each party has is sufficient as a basis for involvement and intervention. Each person, in other words, has their own community centred on themselves. The degree to which these person-centred networks can be effective, of course, will vary, and some are more skeletal than others, so that additional resources from the wider community may be needed to support these networks in turn.

# Theories related to Restorative Justice

The first writer to create a really integrated and comprehensive model of Restorative Justice was Howard Zehr, firstly in a small pamphlet called 'Retributive Justice, Restorative Justice' (1985), and subsequently in his book Changing Lenses (1990). He represented Restorative Justice as an 'alternative justice paradigm', opposed in all principal respects to the principles underlying legal or retributive justice. His work placed particular stress on benefits to victims and enabling offenders to assume active responsibility for putting right the harm they had caused (both as a matter of natural justice and as having a more profound impact on the offender than simply receiving punishment from the court). The interaction between victim and offender, involving personal reconciliation, atonement and, potentially, forgiveness, was presented as entirely compatible with religious notions (especially, but not only, Christian) and given justification in those terms. The limitations of Zehr's early work were the attachment of Restorative Justice ideas to a single practical innovation, mediation (and a particular manifestation of such practice as represented by the VORPs), and its individualistic emphasis, largely neglecting public interests in crime in favour of the more or less private concerns of the victim and the offender. (In his most recent writings, however, Zehr has adopted a more inclusive focus – a wide-angle lens! – and now stresses the potential variety of processes and the more general community interest – e.g. Zehr & Mika, 1998.)

Zehr 's work was widely influential among the growing cohort of converts to such ideas, being particularly evident in the works of Mark Umbreit (1985) in America and Martin Wright (1991) and John Harding (1992) in Britain. These authors treated Restorative Justice as virtually synonymous with victim-offender mediation and continued the emphasis on private negotiation as a sufficient response to crime. Wright, for instance, presented Restorative Justice as a shift from criminal to civil law. This argument is traditionally backed by reference to an earlier paper by Nils Christie (1977) which treated crimes as conflicts between the parties that had been 'stolen' out of their hands by the State and should be returned to the parties. Christie's ideas were particularly influential in his home country, Norway, where they formed the ideological foundation for the unique Municipal Mediation Boards (Fjaerem, 1996). European theory itself developed predominantly in the direction of 'abolitionism' (Bianchi & van Swaaningen, 1986), a radical rejection of state intervention, under the influence of academics like Christie, Bianchi, and de Haan

(1990), and has only recently embraced the more Anglo-American ideas of Restorative Justice, with the influence of Restorative Justice practitioners in Europe (particularly pioneers like Christa Pelikan in Austria, Ivo Aertsen in Belgium, Bonafe-Schmidt in France, and a number of people in Germany, some of whom directly imported personal experiences in the USA and elsewhere – e.g. Thomas Trenczek, Elmar Weitekamp and Heike Jung).

Wright was also much exercised by the problem of reconciling Restorative Justice procedures (ie, in his case, victim-offender mediation) with the traditional justice system. This issue was made particularly clear by emerging research, such as that in Britain published by the Home Office (Marshall & Merry, 1990), and in America and Europe (e.g. Messmer & Otto, 1992, papers from an international NATO conference in Italy). The relationship between the two approaches was made particularly difficult by the apparent opposition between their underlying principles as represented in Zehr's two paradigms, and by the denial in Restorative Justice of the public -interest dimension. It was at about this time that criticism of the over-individualised nature of Restorative Justice thinking also began to emerge, in particular from Harry Mika (1992) in the USA and Tony Marshall (1994) in the UK. As early as 1987, however, Shonholtz in the USA was advocating community-based justice (with some influence from the European abolitionism movement, which was always chary of the ease with which victim-offender mediation could become incorporated by traditional legal values).

The social dimension of Restorative Justice was given a boost by ideas associated with the group forum approaches of indigenous cultures in North America and Pacific nations (e.g. Consedine, 1995) and formal cultural practices of apology and forgiveness in Japan (Haley, 1988). While there is a large literature on community justice (summarised in Marshall, 1985) which was important in the early days, largely in support of neighbourhood justice centres in the USA and elsewhere, more recently these ideas became associated, almost 29 by accident, with a quite separate thread of criminological thought initiated by John Braithwaite (1989) in Australia. His work had developed the idea of reintegrative shaming, a theory of social control that argued that potential offenders were positively influenced by being shamed by their circle of acquaintances or their own community, but were negatively influenced by the alienative shaming of the state in the form of criminal punishment. He favoured locating social control in the community as far as possible. Several writers saw parallels with Restorative Justice thinking in Braithwaite's work (see especially Dignan, 1994). At about the same time Braithwaite himself began to make the same connections. In more practical terms, Braithwaite reinterpreted the New Zealand family group conferences in terms of reintegrative shaming, and this innovation was introduced experimentally in Australia with an explicit justification in terms of his shaming theory. The shaming idea gained further currency and was introduced even into probation and social work practice with offenders on an ad hoc basis, and was confused with notions of meeting the victim and mediation.

Reintegrative shaming is by no means universally accepted as part of Restorative Justice theory. Many people are unhappy with its overtones, as shaming can easily be misapplied in a negative way. For instance, it goes entirely against the grain of Braithwaite's original ideas for agents of the state to apply reintegrative shaming, as is happening when it is applied in social-work contexts or even in family group conferences run by youth justice workers or the police. There is a basic contradiction in state agencies attempting to engineer a community-based process. While they might go as far as to set up the circumstances, through community involvement, in which reintegrative shaming might occur, whether or not it happens will depend on the individuals involved and so it cannot be used as a rationale for state intervention. In any case, Braithwaite's theory is only one of crime control and prevention, and does not encompass the victim-interests and justice- issues that are primary components of Restorative Justice as a whole (Bazemore, 1997).

As it currently stands, Restorative Justice still lacks a definitive theoretical statement, although works continue to be written that take thinking forward, such as Cragg (1992) and Bianchi (1994). The latter casts prisons in a restorative role (as much for the support and protection of the offender as for public protection). Dignan & Cavadino (1996) have made an attempt to integrate different models of Restorative Justice action. The most comprehensive statement and the one that most recognises the community role in Restorative Justice is contained in a number of brief papers by Kay Pranis (e.g. 1997), which attempt to encapsulate the essence of the more socialised conception of Restorative Justice. Marshall (1991b) represented an early attempt to present Restorative Justice in the context of holistic changes in the structure of community, society and political organisation, a line also followed by Weitekamp (1992).

Whether or not it is capable of becoming more than just a model of practice and becoming a complete theory of justice remains to be seen. The academic development of such a theory is still in the early days of development, particularly in terms of the formulation of a philosophy or 'ethics' of Restorative Justice, in which a number of commentators are currently engaged, such as Rob Mackay at Dundee (e.g. Mackay, 1992), and the Penology and Victimology Research Group at Leuven in Belgium (e.g. Deklerck & Depuydt, 1997).

To practical developments this matters very little, and it may be advantageous that it remains an open model able to accept innovations as they occur, rather than a closed system of thought that might restrict options. It is its ability to absorb many different concerns that gives it appeal, and it is its grounding in successful practice that gives it persuasive justification. In this lies its strength and weakness. There is a grave danger that Restorative Justice may end up being all things to all men and women, concealing important divergences of practice and aim. Marshall (1996) identifies one such major rift between social work-orientated practice and the professional mediation stance.

Although no other criminological or justice theory can be held to underpin Restorative Justice, many academic theories and approaches have been incorporated in, or associated with, it at different stages. Perhaps the most fully compatible, although it is not often referred to in this context (with the exception of Marshall & Merry, 1990, and Haines, 1997), is Hirschi's (1969) control theory, which argues that state intervention cannot replace the power of community ties and community acceptance to control misbehaviour. In many ways Braithwaite's ideas are a re-working of Hirschi, and the latter is similarly restricted in its applicability to Restorative Justice because of its lack of concern with justice per se and victims.

Matza's theory of neutralisation has also been applied to victim-offender mediation (e.g. Mackay, 1988, Marshall & Merry, 1990, and Messmer, 1992). Matza argued that a major element in enabling offenders to commit crime while maintaining a positive self-image was that they employed a number of techniques of neutralisation to dismiss or minimise the effects of their actions ("they can afford it", "they'd never miss it") or to justify their actions ("they asked for it"). A confrontation with the victim makes it difficult to maintain such fictions and makes the offenders face up to the reality of the harm they cause.

Other strands of thought that have impacted on Restorative Justice include abolitionism (Bianchi & van Swaaningen, 1986), which advocates community control in replace of state control; feminist criminology (e.g. Heidensohn, 1986; Pepinsky & Quinney, 1991), which emphasises personal relationships and community ; peace-making (Pepinsky & Quinney, 1991) and conflict resolution theory (Kennedy, 1990; Scimecca, 1991), which both treat crime as a conflict better resolved through participation and voluntary agreement than by dictate.

# REFERENCES

Alder, C & Wundersitz, J (Eds) (1994) Family Conferencing and Juvenile Justice. Canberra: Australian Institute of Criminology.

Assembly of Manitoba Chiefs (1989) Final Submission to the Aboriginal Justice Inquiry. Manitoba: Department of Justice.

Association of Chief Officers of Probation (1996) Probation services and the victims of crime. ACOP.

Audit Commission (1996) Misspent Youth. London: HMSO.

Barnett, R (1977) Restitution: a new paradigm of criminal justice. Ethics 87:4, pp 279–301.

Bazemore, G (1997) After shaming, whither reintegration: Restorative Justice & relational rehabilitation. In Bazemore, G & Walgrave, L (Eds) Restoring Juvenile Justice. Amsterdam: Kugler.

Bazemore, G & Griffiths, CT (1997) Conferences, circles, boards, and mediations: the "new wave" of community justice decision-making. Federal Probation 61:2, pp 25–37.

Bianchi, H (1994) Justice as Sanctuary: toward a new system of crime control. Bloomington: Indiana University Press.

Bianchi, H & van Swaaningen, R (Eds) (1986) Abolitionism. Amsterdam: Free University Press.

Bowen, H (1997) Restorative Justice in Aotearoa/New Zealand. ICCA Journal on Community Corrections 8:2 pages 41–45.

Braithwaite, J (1989) Crime, Shame and Reintegration. Cambridge: Cambridge University Press.

Brown, RJ & McElrea, FWM (Eds) (1993) The Youth Court in New Zealand: a new model of justice. Auckland: Legal Research Foundation.

Christie, N (1977) Conflicts as property. British Journal of Criminology 17, pp 1–15.

Christie, N (1982) The Limits of Pain. Oxford: Martin Robertson.

Community Justice Centres (1997) Annual Report 1996–97. New South Wales: CJC.

Consedine, J (1995) Restorative Justice: healing the effects of crime. Lyttelton, NZ: Ploughshares Publications.

Cragg, W (1992) The Practice of Punishment: towards a theory of Restorative Justice. London: Routledge.

Crawford, A (1997) The Local Governance of Crime: appeals to community & partnership s. Oxford University Press.

Davis, G, Boucherat, J & Watson, D (1988) Reparation in the service of diversion: the subordination of a good idea. Howard Journal 27:2.

de Haan, W (1990) The Politics of Redress. London: Unwin Hyman.

Deklerck, J & Depuydt, A (1997) An ethical approach to crime prevention. European Journal on Criminal Policy & Research 5:3 pp 71–80.

Dignan, J (1992) Repairing the Damage. University of Sheffield.

Dignan, J (1994) Reintegration through reparation: a way forward for Restorative Justice? In Duff, Marshall, Dobash & Dobash (Eds) Penal Theory & Practice. Manchester University Press.

Dignan, J & Cavadino, M (1996) Towards a framework for conceptualising and evaluating models of criminal justice from a victim's perspective. International Review of Victimology 4, pp 153–182.

Dignan, J, Sorsby, A & Hibbert, J (1996) Neighbour Disputes. University of Sheffield.

Fjaerem, A (1996) The Norwegian system of mediation boards. Paper to Council of Europe Committee of Experts on Mediation in Penal Matters. Strasbourg: Council of Europe.

Haines, K (1997) Some principled objections to a Restorative Justice approach to working with juvenile offenders. Paper to the First International Conference on Restorative Justice for Juveniles, Leuven, 14 May.

Haley, J (1988) Confession, repentance and absolution. in Wright & Galaway, op.cit.infra.

Harding, J (1982) Victims and Offenders: needs & responsibilities. London: Bedford Square Press.

Heidensohn, F (1986) Models of justice: Portia or Persephone? International Journal of the Sociology of Law 14, pp 287–298.

Hirschi, T (1969) Causes of Delinquency. Berkeley: University of California Press.

Home Office (September 1997a) Getting to Grips with Crime: a new framework for local action: a consultation document. London: Home Office.

Home Office (September 1997b) Getting to Grips with Crime: a new framework for local action: examples of local authority partnership activity. London: Home Office.

Home Office (November 1997) No More Excuses – a new approach to tackling youth crime in England and Wales. London: Home Office.

Hudson, J, Morris, A, Maxwell, G, & Galaway, B (Eds) (1996) Family Group Conferences: perspectives on policy & practice. Willow Tree Press.

Jubilee Policy Group (1992) Relational Justice: a new approach to penal reform. Cambridge: JPG.

Kennedy, LW (1990) On the Borders of Crime: conflict management and criminology. London: Longman.

Lupton, C (1998) User empowerment or family self-reliance? The family group conference model. British Journal of Social Work 28, pp 107–128.

Mackay, R (1988) Reparation in Criminal Justice. Edinburgh: SACRO.

Mackay, R (1992) A humanist foundation for restitution. Paper to Fulbright Colloquium, University of Stirling.

Marshall, TF (1985) Alternatives to Criminal Courts. Aldershot: Gower.

Marshall, TF (1987) Mediation: new mode of establishing order in schools. Howard Journal 26.

Marshall, TF (1991a) Victim-offender mediation. Home Office Research Bulletin 30, pp 9–15.

Marshall, TF (1991b) Criminal Justice in the New Community. Paper for British Criminology Conference, York.

Marshall, TF (1992) Community Disorder & Policing. London: Whiting & Birch. Marshall, TF (1994) Grassroots initiatives towards Restorative Justice. In Duff, Marshall, Dobash & Dobash op.cit.supra.

Marshall, TF (1996) The evolution of Restorative Justice in Britain. European Journal on Criminal Policy & Research 4:4 pp 21–43.

Marshall, TF (1997a) Seeking the whole justice. In Hayman, S (Ed) Repairing the Damage: Restorative Justice in action. London: ISTD.

Marshall, TF (1997b) Criminal justice conferencing calls for caution. Mediation (2 parts).

Marshall, T & Merry, S (1990) Crime and Accountability. London: HMSO.

McAra, L & Young, P (1997) Juvenile justice in Scotland. Criminal Justice 15, pp 8–10.

McCold, P & Stahr (1996) Bethlehem Police Family Group Conferencing Project. Paper to American Society of Criminology Annual Meeting, Chicago, November.

McCulloch, H (1997) Shop theft: improving the police response. London: Home Office: Police Research Group, paper 76.

McElrea, FWM (1994) The New Zealand Youth Court: a model for development in other courts? Paper for the National Conference of District Court Judges, 6–9 April.

Mediation UK (1996) Directory of Mediation Projects & Conflict Resolution Services. Bristol: Mediation UK. Messmer, K (1992) Communication in decision-making about diversion and victim/offender mediation. In

Messmer & Otto, op.cit.supra. Messmer, K & Otto, H (Eds) (1992) Restorative Justice on Trial. Rotterdam: Kluwer.

Mika, H (1992) Mediation interventions and Restorative Justice: responding to the a structural bias. In Messmer & Otto, op.cit.supra.

Morris, A & Maxwell, G (1998) Understanding reoffending. Criminology (New Zealand) 10, pp 10–13. Morris, A, Maxwell, G & Robertson, J (1993) Giving victims a voice. Howard Journal 32:4.

NACRO (1997) A New Three Rs for Young Offenders: responsibility, restoration & reintegration. London: NACRO.

Pepinsky, H & Quinney, R (Eds) (1991) Criminology as Peacemaking. Bloomington: Indiana University Press.

Pranis, K (1997) Communities and the justice system – turning the relationship upside down. VOMA Quarterly 8:1, pp 7–10.

Pranis, K (1997) Rethinking community corrections: restorative values and an expanded role for the community. ICCA Journal on Community Corrections, 8:1, pages 36–39.

Quill, D & Wynne, J (1993) Victim & Offender Mediation Handbook. Leeds: Save the Children.

Sampson, RJ, Raudenbush, SW & Earls, F (1997) Neighborhoods and violent crime: a multilevel study of collective efficacy. Science 277, pp 1–7.

Scimecca, JA (1991) Conflict resolution and a critique of "Alternative Dispute Resolution". In Pepinsky & Quinney, op.cit.supra.

Shonholtz, R (1987) The citizen's role in justice. Annals of the American Academy of Political & Social Science.

Strang, H (1997) Community conferencing: does it work? RISE Project, Canberra, Australia. Paper to Conference on "Calling Young Offenders to Account", London, October.

Umbreit, M (1985) Crime & Reconciliation. Nashville: Abingdon Press.

Umbreit, M (1994) Victim Meets Offender. Monsey, NY: Criminal Justice Press.

Umbreit, M & Coates, R (1992) Victim Offender Mediation: an analysis of programs in four states of the US. Minneapolis: Minnesota Citizens' Council on Crime & Justice.

Umbreit, M, Coates, R & Roberts, A (1997) Cross-national impact of Restorative Justice through mediation and dialogue. ICCA Journal on Community Corrections 8:2 pages 46–50.

Umbreit, M & Roberts, A (1996) Mediation of criminal conflict in England. St Paul MN: Center for Restorative Justice & Mediation.

Utting, D (1996) Reducing criminality among young people: a sample of relevant programmes in the United Kingdom. Home Office Research Study 161. London: Home Office.

Van Ness, DW (1997) Legal issues of Restorative Justice. In Bazemore & Walgrave, op.cit.infra.

Warner, S (1993) Making Amends. Aldershot: Avebury.

Weitekamp, E (19 92) Reparative justice : towards a victim oriented system. European Journal on Criminology, Policy & Research 1:1, pp 70–93.

West, T (1997) Prisons of Promise. Winchester: Waterside Press.

Wright, M (1991) Justice for Victims and Offenders. Milton Keynes: Open University Press.

Wright, M (1997) Some questions answered about FGCs. Family Group Conferences & Youth Justice 2, pp.2 –3.

Wright, M & Galaway, B (Eds) (1988) Mediation & Criminal Justice. London: Sage.

Wynne, J & Brown, I (1998, forthcoming) Can mediation help stop offending? Probation Journal, March.

Zehr, H (1985) Retributive Justice, Restorative Justice. Elkhart: Mennonite Central Committee US Office of Criminal Justice.

Zehr, H (1990) Changing Lenses. Herald Press. Zeh r, H & Mika, H (1998) Fundamental concepts of Restorative Justice. Contemporary Justice Review 1, pp 47–55.